A CLOSER WALK WITH HAPPINESS

Daily "aha" inspirations to help you stay committed to being happy

Tiffany K. Edmonds

A CLOSER WALK WITH HAPPINESS
by Tiffany K. Edmonds

Copyright 2019 by Tiffany K. Edmonds

ISBN: 978-1792669897

Graphic Design: Katie Brady Design
Photographer: Clark Bailey Media

Honor

Before I dedicate this book, I want to give God glory for allowing me to impact the world in this capacity. He's the one that causes me to believe I can do, be, and have all that I that I desire to do, be, and have. I am honored that He chose me for this assignment, and so I give the honor back to God for it truly belongs to Him.

Dedication

To my loving husband of 18 years, Eric and our two beautiful children, Taesia and Titus, you all keep me living, loving, laughing and HAPPY. Thank you for allowing me to be who I am and supporting me through it all. I wouldn't want to do life with any other crew. I love you.

To everyone that has believed in me, prayed for me, encouraged me and supported me, this book is dedicated to ALL of you. You played a major role in the release of this book, and I am so grateful. Thank you from the bottom of my heart.

A Note From
The Happy Chic

You govern your life by the words you speak. I believe that words are powerful and thoughts provoke the words that we speak. I am very adamant about speaking life into the atmosphere. Every since I can remember, I have been good with supporting, encouraging, edifying, and building up others. When social media came on the scene years ago, of course, I started using that platform to speak things that would be on mind or in my heart. I had no idea that it would turn into such an opportunity to share with an even broader audience. So many people have shared how much my words inspired, encouraged and/or motivated them. Several of those same people sent me messages with the idea of having my own daily inspirational journal. These confirming messages began to awaken the idea of having my own book. So here I am!

In these pages you will find daily opportunities to speak life into every day situations, dream again and be reminded to allow your thoughts to shape your world. Yes, that's right, your thoughts. Every word is a thought first. If I can help you change your thought pattern, I can help you change your life pattern. You can speak life, or you can speak death. You can think yourself sad or think yourself happy. Allow these thought provoking "aha" nuggets to encourage you and push you to a place where your eyes are opened to the possibilities that lie dormant within you. It's always time for you to be committed to your happiness.

"A **new year** doesn't mean a **new thing** for **you**, unless you **change** the way you **think**. Is what you're **thinking** today going to push **you** into a better **tomorrow?**"

January 2............................

"When you **finally** start, you're going to see how **close** you are to **finishing**."

" Don't be **intimidated** by your **dreams;** find **ways** for **them** to come to **reality."**

"Just because you're **committed** doesn't mean you **don't feel** like **quitting**. It means **you** fight to **not** quit."

"The **day** you understand how **powerful** choice is, is the **day** you **understand** how powerful **you are.**"

"**Happiness** is not the absence of **difficult times,** it's the **attitude** that difficult **times** won't leave you **absent**."

"Don't let your **feelings** out perform your **faith."**

January 8.................

"Love the **life** you're in! Love the **skin** you're in! **Stop** comparing your **life** with **others**. You have the grace for your **life."**

"Sometimes **waiting** poses itself as **patience** when indeed it's **fear**, especially when it comes to **your dreams** and **desires**. Are you **waiting** or **fearing** to move?"

January 10...................

"A dream is only as **powerful** as the **hands** it's in.**"**

"**Arise!** Shake **yourself** and show the **world** you're still here. "

January 12.................

"Don't shut **down!** There is a **strength** in you to **endure** this.**"**

"Ask with
a **yes**
expectation.**"**

January 14......................

"If you **don't deal** with it immediately, it will **deal** with you **internally**.**"**

"**Smiling** doesn't mean you don't **go** through and **going** through doesn't mean you **can't smile**."

January 16..................

"Being happy takes effort and **intention."**

"How **long** will you be **bitter** over **someone** who's living their **sweet** life?"

January 18..............

"High **five** the person in the **mirror** and say, "You can **make** it", "You can **handle** it", "You were **built** for this", and "You **got** this"."

"Divorce yourself from the **opinion** of your **circumstances."**

January 20............

"**Life** can leave you **numb**, but you must be determined to **feel** again."

"You are good for it! Stop underestimating your purpose and what you bring to the table."

January 22...............

"Don't let the process **steal** the **glory** moment of the **promise."**

"Don't let what you **go** through, **go** through you. Find a **safe** haven. **Release**!**"**

"God is greater than the thing that has you in tap out position. Don't tap out!"

"What are you **willing** to **do** about what **you're** asking **God** to do for **you?"**

"If an **excuse** can **keep** you **from it**, then it's **really** not in you to **do** it. What's in you **comes** out. If **action** is in you, action will come out. If **excuses** are in you, excuses will **come out**."

"Life can **throw** punches at your **faith.** Punch **back!"**

January 28................

"**Whatever** has you **down** and **out** doesn't have the **right** to. Snatch your good **emotions** back!!!"

" Why are you **down** in the **dumps**? Allowing **sorrow** and pity to **lead** you. Get your **head** up. The **Lord** is the right **amount** of anything you will ever **need**. **"**

Psalm 16:5 TKV

January 30................

"When you're **ready**, all **things** will be in place. **God** already knows. The people are within your **reach** and in your **circle** already to **get** it done."

"**Fear** is a time waster. **Think** about what you could have **accomplished** by now if **fear** had not been a **factor**."

"In all your getting, don't forget **God."**

February 2...................

"The Distance Between Your Vision And Your Manifestation Is Your Action... Go The Distance."

"**Stop** looking like **your facts** and **start** looking like your **faith**."

"If you always **follow** people, you will be all **over** the **place**. If you **follow God**, you will **always** be where **you're** supposed to **be."**

"It doesn't take **God** long to **lead** us; it just **takes** us long to **settle** ourselves to hear his **direction."**

February 6...................

"Attraction
excites **you**;
dedication
keeps you.**"**

"Don't **question** how **you're** going to **make** it, just **know** that **you** will."

February 8..................

"Change just needs **somebody** who wants it.**"**

"God is way better than any worse you will ever face."

February 10..................

"I already see the day you thought you would never face. Guess what? You made it through."
~God

"The **quickest** way to get **free** is to be **honest** with **where** you **are**."

February 12.................

"Until **you** get **intentional** about **it,** it won't **happen** on **purpose.**"

"Stop overthinking what God told you to do. Just do it!"

February 14...............

"**Out** of **all** the **bad things** going on **around** you, **don't** take your **eyes** off the **good**. Bad will never outweigh **God's** good for **you**."

"Your **happiness should** be **non negotiable."**

February 16..................

"Your **trial** has a **glory moment** assigned to it. **Keep walking** in **integrity**."

"You can't **finish** a **thing** until you **start** a **thing**."

February 18...................

"**Everybody** attracted to **you** isn't **meant** to be **attached** to you. Rightly **divide**."

"**You** don't
have to **look** like
what you **need**."

"You can't hold on to **familiar** when unfamiliar **territory** has **your name** on it.**"**

"Your response reveals your faith."

"The joy of the Lord is everything I need to get me through any weak moment the enemy tries to introduce to me"

—Nehemiah 8:10 TKV

"Think yourself beyond this trying moment. This moment is not your forever. Live Happy!"

"Speak life into the **atmosphere** and **override** every **negative** thing that has **ever** been **spoken** over **you."**

"Don't ever doubt the resilience that is within you."

February 26.................

"Be encouraged! His strength embraces your weakness."

"Make **God**-decisions **today** that will **lead** to a better **tomorrow**."

"**You** don't **need** anybody's **permission** to be **great**."

"The **enemy** wants **you** to **feel** like **you're** nothing to **keep** you doing **nothing!** **You** are existing for **something**."

"**You** won't **know** where you **really** stand **until** you **eliminate** the **excuses**."

"Your faith causes the enemy to shake in his boots."

March 4.....................

"You have the
God right to
be happy."

"When **you** become **unhindered**, unbothered, and **uninterested** in what **people** have to say about **you**, that's when **you** will **begin** to **shine** and be who **God** has called **you** to be."

March 6.....................

"Have **your moments;** don't **let** them have **you.**"

"**Not** now doesn't **mean** not **ever**."

"Be determined to live the abundant life that's been laid out for you. You're entitled to it."

"The ultimate challenge **winner** resides **within you**, and **He's** handing **out** wins. **Victory** is for **you**."

March 10...................

"When **love** is **there,**
it **doesn't** matter
who's not."

"You won't see the end if you quit."

March 12..........................

"**SHINE** so others will **know** that they **can**."

"When you stop trying to be somebody else, you will be you."

March 14...................

"**You** made it **through** the **night**. Whatever **issues** and **challenges** your **night** consisted of, **YOU** MADE IT!! **Today's** a new **day**."

"The **struggle** may be **real**, but **God** is too. **Don't** forget the **latter**."

"Don't allow **offense** to **make** a **bed** in the **house** of your **heart."**

"Believe you deserve it. You may have gotten some things wrong. You may have messed up a time or two. But there are some things that you have labored for. You deserve your rewards."

March 18..................

"Wake up! **Go** and **work** towards **your** dream **today**.**"**

"**You** may look **crazy** through the **process** but the end **results** will be **worth** it. **Walk** it out. **Your** looking **good days** are **ahead**."

"What God says about **you** should be the **sum total** of what **you** think about **yourself."**

"Don't wait until you need a break to take a break."

"Lord you **have** the **qualities** required to be **God** and your **mercy** remains **in existence** endlessly.**"**

—Psalm 100:5 TKV

"You may **not** understand **everything God** tells **you** to do, but **you** must **understand** that **doing** what **He** tells **you** to **do** is **vitally** important for your **life**."

March 24.....................

"The **thought** of **you** wouldn't let **Jesus** stay in the **grave**. He **got** up for **you**.**"**

"The **enemy** is **counting** on **you** not to be **happy**; show **him** that he can't **count**."

March 26.......................

"Your **participation**
will determine **your** results.
The **ball** is in your **hands**,
make the **play** and decide
to **participate!**"

"Being **faith-filled** is energy. **Being** faithless is **exhausting**."

March 28..................

"It's a **new day** completely **wrapped** in **grace** and mercy. **Seize** it!**"**

"Keep your eyes focused on God, who writes the beginning and end of your faith. The one who thought of you [while His son was on the cross] and still endured the cross [for you before you were born]."

—Hebrews 12:2 TKV

March 30.....................

"No **matter** what happens in **your** life, God is still God!!!!! Our **issues**, challenges, **circumstances**, problems, **let downs**, etc. do **not**, in **any way**, change **GOD's** status."

"Receive what **you're** supposed to **receive** from those around **you**. So when it's **your** time to **pour out**, you will **have** something to **give**."

"God wants **your** life to be **filled** with his **wisdom**."

April 2................................

"No **Thing** Is **Too** Anything for **God**. Amazing **God** = Amazing possibilities!"

"Don't **allow** your **circumstances** to create **excuses** for **you**.**"**

April 4.........................

"Have confidence in change!!! You can handle it."

"If **you** think you've **done** all you **could** do, you **wouldn't** be here. **There's** more. **Dig** deep."

April 6......................

"**Make** a move **towards** your **dream** that **would** be **absolutely** insane for you to **walk** away from. **You** need a **good** "point of **no return**" move."

"In the midst of chaos, listen to the voice of reassurance."

> "You deserve what you desire. Why not you?"

"Being **happy** is **one** of the **greatest** accomplishments **you** can **make**.**"**

April 10.......................

"Dreamers are **not afraid** to make requests. **"Yes" places** await you.**

"**Movement** is vital. **Stuff** begins to **fall** off and/or **fall** into **place** once there is **movement**. Get **unstuck!**"

"**Faith** is **not** the **absence** of pain or **discomfort**. It is the presence of **assurance** that **we** can **live** **through** it."

"Don't **respond** when you're **upset**. You're **never** thinking **clearly** when you're angry. **Wait!!** An angry **response** is **never** an emergency. It can **Wait!!**"

"Everything doesn't work for everybody. Be ok with what works for you."

"Don't be
phenomenal on stage
and phenomenothing
when you're alone."

April 16................

"When **things** and **people** speak contrary to your **vision**, stay **focused**. What did **God** say? **Distractions** are not good **buddies** with **vision**."

"Don't manipulate the process to rush the vision. Be still and know that it will manifest."

April 18...........................

"A **vision** doesn't **exempt** you from **process**; it **keeps** you focused through the **process."**

"You're responsible for you and your happiness; release others of that weight. If you're not happy, look within."

April 20......................

"Let **God** become **apparent** and let **his** enemies be **thrown** quickly in **random directions** [away from **me**]."

—Psalms 68:1 TKV

"God makes you **adequate."**

"Don't be
somebody to everybody
and be **nobody**
to **yourself."**

"Take care
of **yourself!**
You matter.**"**

"**God** created you **happy**. I'm not sure **who** has **convinced** you otherwise. When **God** does a **thing**, he **does** it well."

"Don't allow **your** need to **keep** you from **looking** blessed. **Your** next **blessing** just may be **attracted** to your **presentation**."

April 26...........................

"Your **spotlight** is **nothing** if your **life** light is **dim**."

"**Selfie:** self care, **self love**. Take a **second** to capture **your** beauty or the **moment** you're in. It's **okay** to be **you** and **adore** you."

April 28.........................

"**You** are **enough,** your **voice** matters, and your **life matters.**"

"Identify where **you** are so **you** can get to **where** you're **going**."

"Today, laugh out
loud because you can.
You possess joy;
it's in you."

"Your **overthinking** will **drown** out your **faith.**"

May 2......................

"**Embrace** what **God** created **you** to **be**, not **what** your situation has **made** you **become.**"

"Work **smarter** not **harder**. Don't **complicate** life.**"**

May 4...........................

"**Hello!** You are **not** forgotten. Your **life** is **worth** it; you **can** make it **today**."

"There's no stronghold greater than God. What you're experiencing now doesn't have to last."

May 6........................

"**Death** and **life** ride on the **waves** of your **words**. Watch your **mouth** because **you** will surely **see** the **fruit** of your **words**."

—Proverbs 18:21 tkv

"Remember when you're at your lowest, the highest One is with you. God is the most high."

May 8...........................

"You ought to **step** into your **future** and give **God** a high **five** because you **made** it.**"**

"People will tell you to run and won't even show up to watch you in the race. Don't let that stop you. Keep running."

"God never disappoints. Put that on repeat all day today."

"Gratitude shifts the **attitude!!!** Angry? Sad? Disappointed? Other? Think of something to be grateful for. Make an **exchange** for the joy of the **Lord**."

"If **you** have **stopped** desiring **more**, you have **allowed** less to **capture** your **dreams**."

"There will **always** be something **to** get **you** off track. Stay **Focused!"**

May 14.........................

"Change your **mind**
and **you** will
change your **life!"**

"Your impact is directly connected to your increase. Make an impact today that people won't forget."

May 16.............................

"Sometimes a loss
makes way for your
best win."

"The **more** people **you** push **forward**, the more **hands** you will **have** to pull **you** through **when** you **need** it."

May 18......................

> **"I** can **perform** and achieve the **extent** of any **particular** thing through **Christ** that **makes** me **strong**.**"**
>
> —Phil 4:13 TKV

"Disbelief numbs you to the feeling of hope. Get your spirit up. Believe again."

May 20.........................

"Write your troubles a "Dear John" letter. By the time they read it, you will be gone. Gone with your life and living it abundantly."

"**You** will never **know** the **measure** of negativity a **person** receives on a **daily** basis. Your **ounce** of positivity could **shift** their whole day. **Speak** life. Say something nice. Be **positive**."

May 22...........................

"Everyday, **God** is **speaking** and teaching **you**. Just be **quiet** and **listen**."

"**When** you're in **need**, let **people** help. That's how you will SEE **God's** hand **towards** you."

May 24...........................

"No one will **know** what's on the **inside** of you **unless** you **produce** it. Who will **know** you're an **artist**, if you **never** pick up a **pen** and **draw**. **Who** will know you're a **baker**, if you **never** bake. Who **will** know unless you **produce** it?"

"Don't ever let what you go through drown out the voice of God; you just might miss your breakthrough moment."

"Sharpen your thought life by feeding your mind with positive confessions."

"You're **smarter** than your **situation**."

May 28............................

"**You** are an **overcomer!** The plan that the **enemy** had for you didn't **last** long. The time you gave him was **limited**. **GOD** overruled. You came out on **top**. Your **past** is not your **today**."

"**God** gets no **glory** when **you're** defeated. He **wants** to see you **victorious**."

"Laugh out loud today on purpose; allow joy to increase your day."

"To thine ownself,
be who God told
you to be."

"The **key** ingredient to **where** you **need** to be in **life** is following **God's** lead."

"You've been upset too long. You've been hurt too long. You've been sad too long. It's not doing anything but causing mental and physical turmoil for you. You have the remote for your life in your hands. Turn the channel to happy."

"Get your life back. It's doable."

June 4......................

"Keep **calm** even **when** it **doesn't** go as **planned.""**

"Go through **every** thing with **Victory,** Joy and **Peace!"**

"**When** you **feel** like
you can't **go** on,
keep **living** and **you**
will **discover** that you
actually can. **You** will
look **back** and say,
"Yeah, I **made** it"."

> "Just live one day at a time. Don't worry about tomorrow. Live today."

"Dear Me, Dear Life, Dear Situation, Dear Whatever, I'm committed to my happiness. Sincerely, Me"

"You are fierce and unshakable!!!"

June 10...........................

"In **order** for your **dreams** to **become** a reality, **you** have to **wake** up and **make** it **happen**."

"The **Lord** has already **written** the **script** for your life. **Study** your character. **There's** no **competition** for the **leading** role. **You** are it. Just **follow** the script, learn your lines, and **action!!!**"

June 12......................

"Don't **stop** pursuing your **dreams**. The **people** who mean you **good** will **outweigh** the people who mean **you** bad. Just **stick** with **God** through it all. You've got **this!**"

"Build a relationship with God and His Word that situations, hard times, and challenges can't sabotage."

June 14...........................

"If God is for **you**, he will **show** you **who's** not.**"**

"Cheer up! You're **blessed** and **highly** flavored. **God** seasoned the **world** with the right **pinch** of **you**. **"**

"People are attracted
to authenticity.
Be **true**, be **real**,
and be **you**."

"See **God** in every thing!!!! **After** all, he's there."

June 18..........................

"The **producing**
zealous **prayers** of the
righteous **help** a lot.**"**

—James 5:16 TKV

"**What** you **practice** is what **you** will **produce**."

"There is only one you. God knew one of you would be enough. No one can be you and you can't be anyone else."

"Life will always present something to make you complain about, but it's up to you to decide if you're going to complain or find a reason to be grateful."

June 22.......................

"Don't **draw** back. Lean in with a **mindset** of **victory**. Go face-to-face, toe-to-toe with **whatever** is **hindering** your progress. **Lean** in for the **win**. The finish **line** is where **you** say **it** is."

"If **you** keep **God** in view, you will **keep** things in the **right** perspective."

June 24......................

"Be **encouraged** in being **you**. Just as **soon** as someone **questions** what you **do**, another will **come** along and **compliment you** for **doing** it. Remember, most **things** in **life** are a **matter** of opinion; **embrace** yours."

"Be **God** focused on **purpose**. Stick with **God** like **glue**."

June 26.........................

"When plans change, change plans."

"When life happens, **remember** that **you** were **built** to make it through **anything."**

June 28......................

"**Results** are at
the **end** of your
follow through."

"You are the **key ingredient** to your **happiness."**

"Your **happiness** has to
be **important** you.
Don't be **willing**
to **give** it up for
anybody or anything."

"Don't get so caught up in what you Do that you forget what you Be."

July 2

"**Being** you is the **best** great **you** can **be**."

"Laugh more;
live longer."

July 4............................

"God is waiting for you to press play so He can press fast forward."

"Allow your life to be sautéed in peace, love, joy, wisdom and all things good."

July 6.........................

"Being will far outlast doing."

"The Lord is my **Shepherd**; I shall not **lack** or be short of anything **desirable** or **essential**. I shall want for no thing as long as **He**, the **Lord**, is with **me."**

—Psalm 23:1 tkv

"Be around people who are comfortable enough with themselves to let you be you."

"No **matter** what, God is still God. Your situation **does** not and **will** not **change** that."

July 10...............................

"**You** don't **need** an ending to **start**, but **you** need a beginning to **finish**."

"Smile on purpose today; your light is needed."

July 12.........................

"Your life won't move past your thinking. Whatever you think it will be, that's what it will be."

"Results are not for the lazy. You've got to be in hot pursuit of your happiness."

July 14...........................

"**Today** is a **great** day to focus on those **ideas** and **dreams** that **you** have. **Write** it out as if **you** have all you **need** to **make** it happen. Think from the **wealthy** place that you need to make those **dreams** reality."

"The energy you use to think you can't is the same energy you can use to think you can."

July 16...........................

"When **God** places **amazing** people in **your** life, believe **Him**."

"You don't **need** to see the full **thing** now. **Just** get a **silhouette** view of you **being** where you **want** to **be**."

July 18.....................

"**Faith** is the most **important** matter that occupies **space** in your **heart** while you **wait** for the **thing** you've considered **possible** to manifest and it is the **proof** that you **see** it with your **spiritual** eyes **long** before your natural **eyes** see it."

—Hebrews 11:1 TKV

"When you accept that you're good enough to be where you are and to go where you're going, you will walk into every door that's assigned to you."

July 20.........................

"Wake up! Show your circumstance who's the Boss!

"Someone's life depends on **your directions** from the **Lord**. It's time to **do** what He **told** you **to** do."

"**Live** out **loud** because **you** never know **who** is watching and **listening**."

"Love you.
Appreciate you.
Know your worth."

"If you think you've reached your last level of blessings, you've limited God."

"You have the capacity to seat the blessings that are coming to your life."

July 26.....................

"You have to be intentional about shifting your mood, your day, and your atmosphere when it's producing something contrary to good."

"You have the power to pass up anything that you know won't produce the results you want. That includes food, relationships, jobs, etc."

July 28......................

"**Stop** waiting on **people** to **do** something for you that **you** are not **willing** to do for **yourself**."

"No matter what it **looks** like, you **have** a promise of **victory."**

July 30......................

"Life will give you many reasons not to smile, but all you need is just one that does."

"When God created you, he made a genius move."

"You have the ability to change the course of your day by simply taking a moment to exhale gratitude."

August 2...........................

"You are **the** power **source** to your **emotions."**

"**Own** what **God** says **about** you."

August 4..................

"Love you in **every** way **you** can. **Lead** the **way** of self-love.**"**

"Embrace your **flaws** and **just** flow with **them**.**"**

"**Faith** will **always** be miles **ahead** of **your** eyes."

"Don't ever let people make you feel ashamed to live out loud because they're afraid to."

August 8........................

"Every day the Lord
packs my life with
advantages I've gained
because He is
my Savior."

—Psalm 68:19 TKV

"You've got "pull it together" power on the inside of you."

"The phone you're using now is a result of someone's work. The car you drive is the result of someone's work. The job you have is the result of someone's work and so on. You get it? Now, what will someone see, be, do, and/or have as a result of your work?"

"God deals a good hand; even when we don't understand."

"**Rewards** are inevitable for **those** who **do** the **work**."

"Don't **complicate your** life. Take opportunities. If they don't **work**, so what? At least you **tried**."

"If **you** don't **know who** you are, **others** will try to **define** you. If you don't know **whose** you are, **others** will try to **own** you. If you **don't** know **where** you are, **others** will try to **locate** you. **Discover** You!"

"**You** shine **best when** you **reflect** the **Lord's** light."

August 16....................

"**You** are **enough**. You may **not** be **for** everybody **but** for those **you** are called **too**... you are **enough!**"

"Failing means at least you tried. Don't let the fear of failure keep you stuck."

"Do not get exhausted in doing great things for The Lord, for you shall see your stuff if you don't pass out.

—Galatians 6:9 TKV

"Your dream **runs** parallel to **you**. Whatever **you** do, your **dream** will **do**. If you **sit**, your **dream** will sit. If **you** go, your **dream** will go.**"**

"People may **not know** you **personally, but favor does."**

"Don't let your circumstances bully you."

August 22......................

"**Life** is a **photo** booth. Smile, **strike** a pose, **take** a **picture**, and create **memories** that **last**."

"Never let anyone make you feel inferior. You are major!!!"

August 24................................

> **"Inspiration** causes change. Have you **been** inspired **lately?"**

"You have to be **intentional** and unapologetic **about** what you want. Go get it!"

August 26...................

"Just **think** if **you** had started **yesterday**, today **would** be **day** two. Whatever **it** is, **begin**."

"Favor surrounds you like a shield. It's your garment of guarantee. It protects you from the norm. It escorts you to above average and exceptional. It moves you the front of the line. It takes you to yes places."

"**What** do you **do** when something **doesn't** work out? **Work** something else **out**."

"Wake up! Get up! Live up! Someone is waiting on you."

"**You** are **the** perfect canvas **for your** purpose."

"Stay focused! God never stops being good."

"You were not made to do life alone. Get out and connect."

September 2 ....

"Unexpected **blessings** are **hints** from **heaven** that **God** is **paying** attention to **you**."

"Sometimes you need someone to tell you "no" so that you can be your "yes"."

September 4...............

"**Until** your **mind** shifts, your **life** won't change."

"When was the last time you did what makes you happy?"

September 6...............

"**Arise!** Color the
world with
the **beauty** of
your **presence**."

"It **doesn't** matter **what** they **think** you can't do; it **only** matters **what** you think you **can**."

September 8..................

"Hit the **ground** running towards **what** you **want** to see **happen** in your **life."**

"When **people** cut **you** off, take **bow** and exit stage **right**. Your **role** in **that** script is **over**."

September 10................

"**Faith** without **works** is a **graveyard** situation."
—James 2:17 TKV

"We are not **void** of challenges **but** we have been **vested** with **courage** to get through **them**."

September 12...............

"Today set your barometer on happy. Don't let anyone bring your levels down."

"A **mile** is a mile **no** matter how **long** it takes **you** to **get** there. **Pace** yourself for your **goals** and dreams. Your **race**, your **pace!**"

September 14..............

"Concentrating **on God's** love **for** you is key to a sound **life."**

"Get on your mark, mindset, and go. Go and be!"

September 16...............

"Listen to God;
He will tell you
what to do."

"**This** is the **day** that
the **Lord** has made;
catch **up.**"

"We don't walk hand in hand, side-by-side, or toe-to-toe with what we see. We grab hands with faith, stand by its side, and take the same steps it [faith] takes."

—2 Corinthians 5:7 TKV

"Being you will pay off. Stay consistently authentic."

September 20...........

"**Effort** leaves a **trail** of **evidence**. What effort **have** you **put** towards your **happiness.**"

"**Why** not **you?**
You're **surely**
good enough."

September 22...............

"Fall **back** from **worrying** and stressing. Let **God** direct **you!**"

"God always predicts that you win."

September 24................

"Your bad days are at an all time low and very much outnumbered by the goodness the Lord satisfies you with."

"Put forth an effort towards what you want to see happen this year."

September 26...............

"**Don't** wait **until** you **die** to **fly** high; soar **now!**"

"We **tend** to put **limits** on **what** and who we can **forgive** based on **what** happened. As **long** as **we** do **that**, we limit our **freedom**. Forgiveness produces **freedom**."

"Faith is made to extend. Think about it. If faith is always now it's always right where it needs to be. It's always now, for us."

"In all that you do, make sure the Lord gets the glory out of your life."

"Whatever you want in life, believe that you can have it. Believe you have what it takes to get it."

"When you ask God to help you, you have to put forth the effort to be helped."

October 2......................

"Life is too short.
How long will sit
on your dream?"

"Don't give the enemy the pleasure of a win."

"It only takes one person to change your status. You don't need a crowd, just that one person who has the power to catapult you to your next."

"The **enemy** has a **goal** and that is to **maximize** what's **going** wrong so **you** can minimize **what's** going **right**."

October 6......................

"When people don't **need** you **anymore**, shout for **joy**.**"**

"Life Happens;
Live Happy."

October 8..................

"It's a great day to be here! Let hope arise within you. You're here for a purpose. Tap in."

"**Drink** a **cup** of determination **today!**"

"Don't be so consumed with the bad that you question the good."

"**Everything** doesn't require a **response** from **you**. Protect your **peace** and **happiness**."

October 12...................

"**Amazing** is waiting **for** you to put **forth** an effort! **Someone** else's **amazing** will only **get** you so **far** but **your amazing** will take you wherever **you need** to be."

"**Don't** let anyone destroy what's **valuable** to **you** including your **happiness**."

October 14..................

> **"**Go **back** to the **thing** that made **you** doubt **God** and tell that **thing** that **it** was **wrong**.**"**

"Go outside! Take notes from the sun and let your light shine."

"Don't **apologize** for your **journey**; just continue to give **God** the **glory** while **you're** on it."

"If God is for you,
why are you
against you?"

October 18......................

"If **you** don't **act** on what you **believe**, pleasing **God** is not **happening**. When **you** go to the **Father**, you must **believe** [without any doubt] that **He** is [everything] and that He **returns good** for the **evil** [the devil **meant** for you] if you **seek** after him **steadily** with dedication and **persistence**."

—Hebrews 11:6 TKV

"**You** have the **power** to unsubscribe at **anytime** to **anything** that brings you **negativity**."

October 20..................

"Integrity: when it **matters** because **God** sees **you.**"

—Psalms 68:1 TKV

"**You** are **top** priority to **God**."

October 22.....................

"The **longer** you **wait,** **the** longer it **takes** you to **get** there."

"You have a right to see your dreams come to past. Believe that!"

October 24...................

"God will use **people** to pull **purpose** out of you. Get **connected!"**

"When you decide that you want to get back up, you can and you will. You have people rooting for you but you must do the "get up" work."

October 26...................

"Be **encouraged**;
reaping is **inevitable."**

"**What** you're going **through** will **soon** be a **memory**."

October 28..................

"**Put** on a **victory** mindset **that** will **push** **you** forward into **greater** things."

"God has the power to mend every piece of you that has been torn or broken."

October 30..................

"Don't give anything more credit than you give God."

"No **worst** bad **will** ever outweigh God's best **good**. While **living** in this sick, **twisted** and evil world, **don't** you lose **focus** of how so **very** good **God** is."

"When **you** want **God** to **add** to your **life**, you have to be **willing** to subtract what doesn't **belong**."

November 2................

"**Don't** you **dare** let the **process** wear **out** your **praise**."

"God has a lifetime of manifestations assigned to your life."

November 4...............

"**Reminder!** You're not **what** or **who** you **used** to be."

"Listen to God. He's got the "one step away" answer you need."

November 6..................

"When are you
going to let your
purpose live?"

"No situation in your life is too heavy for God to lift."

November 8 . . . .

"Nothing we **go** through changes **or** limits **God."**

"Don't settle; tell your circumstances to shut up."

"You are not subject to your **challenges** and **issues**; they **must** take **heed** to the **Word** you **declare**."

"It is **impossible** for **God** to fail **you**."

"No **matter** what **it** looks like, God is good. **Don't** let **your** situation rob **you** of that **fact**."

"It doesn't matter how you got in it, God has a way to get you through it."

November 14...............

"**Keep** your **eyes** set above **what** you **can** see. What you **see** is **not** all **that** you **will** be."

"Don't **forget** about your **dreams** and **goals**; you are still alive **today** to start **working** on them."

November 16..................

"Your story, your journey is the "aha" moment someone else may need to complete their story or their journey."

"Change comes with growth. Are you changing? Are you growing?"

November 18..................

"We **always** want
more with our **mouths**,
but our **minds**
are **stuck** on **less**."

"Don't have a loaded hand and an empty heart. Get your heart full first or else what's in your hands won't do much for you."

November 20..............

"Stop **settling** for
the **struggle**.**"**

"One of the worst things we can do is to fight against what God created us to do and to be."

"You can't grab hold to what God has for you if you're afraid to let go of what's not for you."

"If you're **waiting** for the **numbers** to be great, you're not **ready** to **do** what God told **you**."

November 24................

> **"God** uses **people.**
> Can He **count** on
> **you?"**

............November 25

"In the **thick** of **things**, don't **thin** your **faith**."

"God knows exactly what you don't know yet. Follow his lead."

"**Don't** allow **lack** to **keep** you from **showing** up to **get** your **increase**."

"Starting is the quickest way to finishing."

"Being you will take you places way faster than being someone you're not."

November 30...............

"If things never went wrong, we would never explore other options. Sometimes other options work out better than the first ones."

> **"Let** there be **life** in **all** that **you** do.**"**

December 2.................

"**Dreams** do **come** true, **if** you **come** through. Do your **part**."

"**Don't** let **rejection** be the **end** you."

December 4 . . . .

"When the enemy comes in like a flood, sail like a boss because the Lord rolls with you.

—Isaiah 59:19 TKV

"Feeling like you're not good enough is a distraction that detours you from destiny."

December 6..................

"You have God's permission to be great. So, go ahead and be great."

"God needs you so he can show the world He's tangible."

December 8..................

"No **matter** what **seems** to be a **shock** or surprise to **you**, it's **never** that to God. Nothing catches **Him** by **surprise**."

"Praise and gratitude give your manifested blessing permission to enter into the doors of your life."

"Sometimes it's not that we don't hear God; it's that sometimes our circumstances and doubt speak louder."

"Don't **hate** the **player**; ask **them** how **they** did it."

December 12...............

> "**Small** steps **lead** to bigger **strides.** **Start** somewhere."

"Time will **tell** what you **won't**. Time **always** reveals **results** or the lack **thereof**."

December 14...............

"**Everything** you need is **within** reach, but **you** won't **know** that until you **reach**...out. Asking is **key**."

"Encouragement can save a life. Do it more; you never know the impact."

December 16..............

"Being **impatient produces** reckless living and **guarantees** a **frustrated** life."

"Faith puts a **demand** on **the** blessings **that** are **assigned** to your **life."**

December 18...............

"You will **never** be able to **commit** above your **level** of **honesty** with **where** you **are** in your **thinking**.**"**

"Your **story** is a **setup** to help **someone** else **come** up."

December 20.............

"You can't compare your beginning to someone's ending. You will cancel yourself out every time."

"Smile! It can change your mood."

"There are some things that you just won't understand and agree with. Breathe! Consider your response before you react."

"A doer makes **executions;** a don't-er makes **excuses."**

December 24.................

"Your **outcome** is **subject** to **your** confession. **Change** your **confession;** change your **outcome.""**

"Don't be so afraid of messing up that you don't try. Let fear motivate you to at least try."

December 26..............

"Stop! Smell the roses, draw in the sand, etc. Appreciate moments to think of absolutely nothing at all but being at your happiest."

"Whatever you say you can or can't do, will be what you can or can't do."

December 28...............

"Life is better when you believe that it is."

"If you don't **take** care
of **yourself,**
the **grave** will!**"**

December 30...............

> "**Work** what **you** have until **you** have **what** you **want**."

"Everyday, tell yourself to give your dreams one more chance. If you do that, you will never quit."

Made in the USA
Middletown, DE
09 January 2019